S is for Scientists
A Discovery Alphabet

Written by Larry Verstraete and Illustrated by David Geister

For Ashley and Nick—
May great discoveries greet you at every turn in the road ahead.

LARRY

✳

To my high school art teacher, Karl Sakschek—
a friend who guided me and opened my eyes to a world of possibilities.

DAVID

ACKNOWLEDGMENTS

Thanks to my pals Taber, Emma, Rachel, Kunal, Collin, Taylor, Maddie, Luke, and Isaac, all of whom posed for me and made my work easier. The usual, helpful advice and research assistance was given by my comrade, Aaron Novodvorsky. And, as always, I am most grateful to my dear wife, Patricia Bauer, the keeper of sanity when there is never enough time in the day.

—David

This book would not have been possible without the dedication of scientists past and present. To them I owe a hearty round of gratitude. Thank you as well to my enthusiastic high school chemistry teacher, Brother Joseph Yasho, for awakening my interest in the subject. I am also indebted to Dr. Barbara McMillan of the Faculty of Education, University of Manitoba for her advice on several aspects of the book. Last, but not least, thank you to my wife, Jo, as well as family and friends for their unfailing support and encouragement.

—Larry

Sleeping Bear Press™
315 E. Eisenhower Parkway, Suite 200
Ann Arbor MI 48108
www.sleepingbearpress.com

Sleeping Bear Press is an imprint of Gale, a part of Cengage Learning.

Printed and bound in China.

10 9 8 7 6 5 4 3 2 1

Library of Congress Cataloging-in-Publication Data

Verstraete, Larry.
S is for scientists : a discovery alphabet / written by Larry Verstraete ; illustrated by David Geister.
p. cm.
ISBN 978-1-58536-470-1
1. Scientists—Juvenile literature. 2. Alphabet books.
I. Geister, David, ill. II. Title.
Q147.V475 2010
500—dc22   2010010739

In this book
　　　you will find
stories about scientists
　　　with curious minds.

Unraveling puzzles
　　　is what they do
as they search for answers
　　　to how, why, where, who.

What scientists discover
　　　changes us all
and brings more questions—
　　　some big, others small.

So read their stories
　　　and wonder, too.
What questions do *you* have?
　　　What discoveries await *you*?

A a

Splitter splat, the goop fell
splashing on the shoe,
causing Patsy to adapt
her plans of what to do.

While working for the 3M Company in 1953, chemist Patsy Sherman noticed something odd after an assistant dropped a glass beaker on the floor. Sherman had been trying to develop a new kind of rubber for jet aircraft fuel lines and the beaker contained a batch of synthetic latex she had recently produced. It shattered on impact, splashing latex around the room. A glob landed on the assistant's canvas tennis shoe.

To clean the shoe, a number of solvents were tried—water, soap, alcohol. Nothing worked. The liquids bubbled and rolled off the canvas. It was as if the glob had created an invisible barrier impossible for chemicals to penetrate.

Sherman recognized an opportunity in disguise and quickly adapted to the new situation. The latex had unexpected properties, ones she hadn't noticed earlier. With the help of fellow 3M chemist Sam Smith, she ran tests on the substance and fine-tuned its formula.

In 1956, 3M launched Scotchgard®, a new stain-resisting chemical, the product of Patsy Sherman's quick-thinking shift.

Disappointed with their early gliders, brothers Orville and Wilbur Wright retreated to the Dayton, Ohio bicycle shop that doubled as their lab. Out of spare materials, they built a six-foot-long (1.8 meter) wooden box open at both ends. One end they called "goesinta," the other "goesouta." A fan powered by a small gasoline engine at the "goesinta" end swept air into the box while the "goesouta" opening allowed the air to leave. Inside the box, the Wrights fastened a balance made out of a hacksaw blade and a bicycle spoke wire.

Using their homemade wind tunnel, the Wright brothers tested various wing designs by hanging small models inside the box. As air swept over the wings, they measured lift and drag forces with the balance. After viewing the results, they tweaked their designs, adjusting wing shape and size to improve efficiency.

Over a two-month period, the Wright brothers tested more than two hundred wing models. Armed with a better understanding of aerodynamics, they redesigned the glider. In 1903, the Wright brothers made history, achieving prolonged flight with a heavier-than-air machine for the first time in Kitty Hawk, North Carolina, a place with strong, steady winds and flat terrain where they could test their craft safely.

Bb

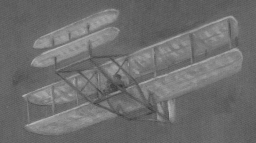

B is for Build

A drafty space, this tunnel
built from scraps of wood and wire,
but the perfect place to test
the Wright brothers' super flyer.

C

C c

In 1929, Clyde Tombaugh, a 22-year-old amateur astronomer, arrived at the Lowell Observatory in Flagstaff, Arizona to begin a time-consuming search. From calculations of Uranus's orbit, astronomers had predicted the existence of a ninth planet at the outer reaches of the solar system. Tombaugh set out to find this mysterious body—the so-called Planet X.

For ten months, Tombaugh photographed the night sky and carefully compared photographs looking for shifts in position that might indicate a moving body. In January 1930, he exposed two photographic plates taken of a region in the constellation Gemini. When Tombaugh compared them later, he noticed a difference—a faint shift of light, a pinpoint dot that had changed location slightly. Immediately, he knew he had found Planet X.

On May 1, 1930, the new body was called Pluto a name suggested by an 11-year-old British schoolgirl. For decades, Pluto was called the ninth planet in the solar system, but in 2006, with the discovery of new bodies in space and a better understanding of Pluto's size and orbit its status was changed. Pluto is now considered to be a dwarf planet rather than a major planet like Mars, Jupiter, and the others. Even so, Tombaugh's sharp-eyed discovery is remarkable by any standard.

C is for Compare

Two photographs compared
    showed a flicker, just a trace—
a pinpoint shift of light,
    the site of Planet X in space.

D is for Demonstrate

Sixteen horses strained and pulled,
putting on a spectacular show,
but air demonstrated super strength
by never once letting go.

Otto von Guericke's device was simple—just two hollow copper bowls—but what the German scientist did with them ranks as one of the most dramatic of all scientific demonstrations.

On May 8, 1654, in front of Emperor Ferdinand III and a crowd of onlookers, von Guericke greased the two bowls and fit them together to form a sphere approximately 20 inches (51 centimeters) in diameter. Using a pump he had invented, he sucked air from the sphere to create a vacuum. Next, von Guericke harnessed two horses to each side. The horses lurched and tugged, but the bowls held tight. Gradually other horses were added—a total of eight on each side at one point according to most reports. Whips snapped, dust flew, the horses pulled, but still the seal held.

Von Guericke's demonstration proved the point he was trying to make: Air exerts tremendous pressure. With air removed from *inside* the sphere, the only force holding the bowls together was the air pressing on the *outside* of the sphere, yet it was enough to defeat a team of horses pulling with all their might.

Dd

In the early 1900s Russian scientist Ivan Pavlov observed something interesting while using dogs in his study of digestion. Normally, the sight or smell of food caused the dogs' salivary glands to go into action, producing drool and beginning the digestive process. But Pavlov noticed that one of the dogs began to salivate even though no food was present.

Pavlov believed that the dog had been *conditioned* to salivate. Because Pavlov's assistants wore white coats during feedings, the dog had unconsciously learned to connect the coat with food. In time, just seeing a white coat was enough to trigger the salivation response.

Pavlov set up a series of experiments where he paired food with various sights or sounds. In one, he rang a bell just before food was delivered. After a few tries, the sound of the bell itself was enough to cause the dog to drool.

Pavlov's study opened the door to other investigations of behavior and laid the foundation for a branch of psychology known as classical conditioning.

Ee

E is for Experiment

In his classic experiment,
Ivan put dogs in the mood
of licking their chops and slobbering,
even without having their food.

F f

Drawn by a tale of long ago,
Hiram Bingham followed the clues
and led the expedition
all the way to Machu Picchu.

In 1911 Hiram Bingham, an American history professor, led an expedition of six men into the jungles of Peru. Bingham had heard stories about a lost city belonging to the Inca, a powerful nation that once lived in Peru's high mountain regions. Drawn by the tales, the men clawed through dense jungle, waded across treacherous streams, and trudged up steep slopes. At each village, Bingham asked the same question: Has anyone seen the ruins of an ancient city?

On July 24 he heard an encouraging answer from one native. The man guided the group along a narrow, twisting trail choked with vines and rocks. Hours later, Bingham found himself at the bottom of a series of stone terraces. A stairway led to a huge courtyard—the entrance to an abandoned ancient city.

Named Machu Picchu (meaning "Old Peak" in the Quechua language), the city was an archeological jewel, a masterpiece of temples, palaces, and homes perched high on the mountain. Although not the same lost city that Bingham hoped to find, Machu Picchu stands as one of the world's great wonders, a tribute to the advanced culture of the Incan people of long ago.

In 1941 American botanist Richard Evans Schultes set off alone into the Amazon rainforest with a small canoe and a backpack containing a notebook, camera, a few cans o food, a change of clothes—and little else. A the time, doctors were interested in *curare* a chemical mixture with muscle-relaxing properties that came from unidentified Soutl American plants. Schultes hoped to track down the sources of curare, identify the plants that provided it, and gather samples for study.

Schultes paddled down remote rivers, explored the dense jungle, and questioned natives he felt might have knowledge about local plants to share. Over a 14-year period he identified and collected more than 70 plant specimens that were sources of curare.

Schultes realized that the Amazon was a rich source of new medicines. During his lifetime, he campaigned to protect the rapidly disappearing rainforest. He also gathered more than 24,000 new plant specimens, of which 120 now bear his name.

G is for Gather

Up the Amazon Richard paddled,
gathering plants, naming flowers,
discovering new medicines
with wonderful healing powers.

H is for Hypothesize

A hypothesis is an educated guess
and Ignaz guessed a whopper
by saying that washing hands
could be an infection-stopper.

In the 1840s Dr. Ignaz Semmelweis noticed a disturbing trend at the hospital where he worked in Vienna, Austria. The death rate in the First Clinic maternity ward where medical students delivered care, was much higher than in Second Clinic where babies were delivered by midwives. *Why*? he wondered. Semmelweis observed the wards and conducted autopsies on the dead, hoping to discover clues.

One day a fellow doctor accidentally cut himself with a scalpel during an autopsy. Even though the cut was minor, the doctor died of symptoms very similar to those of patients who had died in First Clinic. Acting on these observations, Semmelweis tracked movements between wards. Doctors and students, he noticed, often went from the autopsy room directly into First Clinic.

Semmelweis hypothesized that somehow infection was being carried into First Clinic. He announced a new rule: Patients, students, and doctors had to wash and disinfect their hands before moving from one ward to another. Before long, the death rate dropped dramatically, proving what we now take for granted but was unknown then—cleanliness reduces the spread of infection and disease.

I i

For years, scientists Marie Curie and her husband, Pierre, worked with pitchblende, a black mineral ore. Pitchblende had radioactive properties and the Curies hoped to isolate and identify the elements in the compound. An abandoned wooden shed in Paris became their laboratory. There they slaved over hot fires, boiling tons of pitchblende, extracting and filtering the substance, then putting the purified crystals into small glass bowls for further study.

One night in April 1902, Marie felt a nagging urge to return to the laboratory. Accompanied by Pierre, she let herself into the dark shed. A wondrous sight greeted them. From thousands of glass bowls came a strange bluish-purple glow. Dazzled by their beauty, Marie called the crystals her "magical blue glow-worms." The crystals turned out to be radium, a radioactive element.

Early in their work with pitchblende, the Curies noticed something odd. Strange red sores had appeared on Marie's hands. Days afterward the sores mysteriously vanished. Believing that the radium might be the cause, Pierre exposed his arm to radiation from the newfound element. A burn appeared. Weeks later, it too disappeared. They repeated the test on animals, each time with similar results.

I is for Isolate

In the shed, in the dark of night
    a bit of magic, an eerie glow.
Isolated and left alone
    it was radium's dazzling show.

Radiation killed cells, the Curies found, but in time healthy cells replaced the destroyed ones. The discovery led to a new medical treatment. Today, we use radiation as a cancer-fighting weapon. Given in carefully measured doses, radiation kills cancer cells, allowing healthy ones to take their place.

For their discovery of radium, the Curies were awarded the Nobel Prize for physics in 1903, the first time a woman ever received the honor. Constant exposure to radiation, however, weakened Marie and took its toll. In 1934 she died of cancer, the very disease she had sought to conquer.

J j

is for Join

When molecules joined together
in Stephanie's new-fangled brew,
        the mix turned thin and cloudy—
a sure sign of something new.

In the 1960s, Stephanie Kwolek, a chemist for the DuPont Company in Buffalo, New York, was asked to develop a high-performance fiber that could be used to make car tires lighter, stronger, and more fuel efficient.

Kwolek specialized in polymers—compounds made of long chains of molecules joined together. She tried various combinations, mixing one batch of chemicals after another and subjecting them to different conditions of heat and moisture. One day in 1964, she ended up with something odd. Rather than being clear and syrupy like other polymer solutions, this batch was cloudy and thin.

Thinking the solution might be contaminated, Kwolek was tempted to throw it away. Instead, she filtered the liquid and passed it through a spinneret, a machine that forced the solution through tiny holes to produce threads. The results were surprising—a tough, lightweight fiber, nine times stronger and stiffer than any other.

The company dubbed the fiber Kevlar.™ Today, Kevlar™ is used alone or combined with other materials in a range of products where super-strength and durability are needed—everything from skis and tennis racquets to ropes, bullet-proof vests, and fire-resistant clothing.

Marjorie Courtenay-Latimer came to the docks of East London, South Africa on December 23, 1938, to search through the latest catch of fish. Courtenay-Latimer, a naturalist and curator at the East London Museum, was on the hunt for specimens to add to the museum's collection. Finding nothing new, she turned to leave but stopped when she spotted a shiny blue fin jutting from a pile. Digging it out, she discovered what she later called "the most beautiful fish I had ever seen."

It was, in fact, extremely odd—heavily armored, thickly scaled, with fins that were knobby and almost leg-like. Fascinated, Courtenay-Latimer kept the fish. In a reference book, she found an illustration of a similar-looking creature, a prehistoric fish thought to have been extinct for 65 million years.

Later an expert identified the fish as a *coelacanth* (SEE-la-canth), a creature known to science only through its fossils. Courtenay-Latimer's discovery sparked hot debate among scientists who wondered not only how the coelacanth had escaped detection for so long, but also if it might be a missing link in the chain of evolution.

K
k

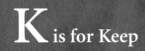

K is for Keep

Treasure worth keeping,
that's what our Marjorie thought
of the strange fish, the armored beast—
the creature that time forgot.

L is for Link

Linking computers together
is mighty easy and quick.
Thanks to Tim's great idea
we can do it with a mouse click.

When documents piled up in his computer, Tim Berners-Lee, a British software engineer, looked for ways to simplify and organize his files. In 1980 he wrote a computer program for himself that connected random bits of information. By linking words in documents to files on his computer and simply keying in a number, his program allowed him to quickly access stored information.

Berners-Lee called the program Enquire. Enquire worked so well that he expanded its use and opened it up to his colleagues at the European particle physics laboratory where he worked. Using his program, workers could access each other's computers and obtain the documents they needed in a speedy, efficient way.

But Berners-Lee didn't stop there. He saw an even brighter future for his system. In 1991, using software Berners-Lee wrote and rules he devised for its use, the World Wide Web became a reality. Today, thanks to his vision, linking computers and transferring ideas around the globe takes little more than a click of the mouse.

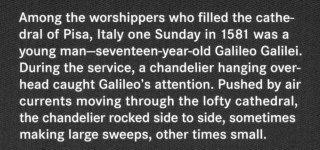

Among the worshippers who filled the cathedral of Pisa, Italy one Sunday in 1581 was a young man—seventeen-year-old Galileo Galilei. During the service, a chandelier hanging overhead caught Galileo's attention. Pushed by air currents moving through the lofty cathedral, the chandelier rocked side to side, sometimes making large sweeps, other times small.

Regardless of the size of the chandelier's arc, it seemed to Galileo that each swing took the same amount of time. Curious, Galileo felt for the pulse in his wrist. Using it as a gauge, he timed the chandelier's movement. One, two, three beats for one swing. One, two, three beats for another. His hunch was right. The times were the same.

After the service, Galileo ran home, rigged up a model "chandelier" using a weight on a string, and took more precise measurements. What started as a distraction in church ended up becoming a landmark event in science. Galileo not only discovered the principle of the pendulum, he also showed that measurement and experimentation could be used to prove natural laws—the basis of the scientific method we use today.

M m

M is for Measure

In a cathedral tall and vast
a chandelier swayed to and fro,
a regular thing, the rhythm of its swing
measured by the pulse of Galileo.

N n

With Ted Fujita's system,
numbers tell a twister's might.
Five for incredibly fearsome,
zero for breezy but light.

Tornadoes are wildly unpredictable, striking hard and fast in such haphazard ways that measuring and tracking them is difficult. In the 1970s our understanding of tornadoes took a giant step forward thanks to Tetsuya Theodore "Ted" Fujita, a professor of meteorology at the University of Chicago. Rather than studying tornadoes directly, Fujita carefully analyzed the damage tornadoes did instead. He examined aerial photographs taken after tornado strikes, did calculations based on the extent of damage, and compared patterns of destruction. From this data, he charted wind speeds and directions.

Fujita concluded that not all tornadoes were alike—a new idea at the time. Some were small and weak, others larger, faster, or more destructive. To tell them apart, Fujita set up a numbering system called the Fujita Scale which ranked tornadoes by linking wind speed to damage. Divided into six categories, weakest to strongest, the F0 to F5 markers of the Fujita Scale gave scientists a much-needed, practical way of determining the strength of tornadoes.

In 1960 Jane Goodall, a British secretary, traveled to the jungles of Tanzania in Africa to begin a study of chimpanzees for Louis Leakey, a noted anthropologist. Untrained in the ways of science, Goodall quietly observed the chimps using methods uniquely her own. Rather than watching from a distance, Goodall lived among the animals, gave them names, and gradually earned their trust and acceptance. Slipping almost unnoticed among the chimps, Goodall made startling discoveries that challenged commonly held beliefs.

Goodall's first discovery came the day she saw a chimpanzee strip the leaves off a twig and shove it into a termite mound to gather insects. Making and using tools were things only humans could do, scientists thought, yet her observation proved that chimpanzees could as well. Another time, a chimpanzee gently took her hand and squeezed it in a gesture of friendship. The simple act revealed depths of emotion which, until then, were thought impossible for animals.

Through patient observation over a period of decades, Jane Goodall has opened our eyes, revealing new possibilities in the ways animals relate to each other and how we relate to them as well.

O is for Observe

In the jungles of Tanzania
    Jane observed the chimpanzees
discovering animal ways
    and great possibilities.

P is for Prove

A flimsy raft made of wood,
the *Kon-Tiki* sailed the sea
braving storms, riding waves,
bringing proof to you and me.

Pp

Just how the Polynesian Islands of the South Pacific became settled was widely discussed among scientists in the 1930s. Many thought that the first inhabitants had come from South Asia and had sailed east across the Pacific Ocean to the Polynesian Islands. Norwegian anthropologist Thor Heyerdahl thought differently.

If early settlers had come from Asia, Heyerdahl reasoned, they would have had to travel *against* the prevailing current, a long and difficult journey. Instead, Heyerdahl believed that the first settlers had come from the opposite direction, from South America, and had sailed west *with* the current to reach Polynesia.

In 1947 Heyerdahl set out to prove that such a journey was possible. Using ancient building methods, he and a crew of five inexperienced sailors lashed together a 35-foot (10.7 meters) raft from balsa logs. Christening the craft *Kon-Tiki*, they set sail from Callao, Peru, aiming their primitive vessel for the Polynesian Islands. Fighting storms, circling sharks and the blistering sun, they made the voyage across the Pacific in 101 days, proving the point that had started the expedition: Polynesia's early settlers could have come from South America aboard similar vessels.

Q is for Question

Questions popped into Percy's head;
he wondered how and why
chocolate could have turned to mush
and eggs could be made to fly.

In 1946 when Percy Spencer, an American engineer, reached into his pocket for a chocolate bar after working on a radar set at the Raytheon Manufacturing Company, he found a melted mess. *Why?* he wondered. The room hadn't been especially warm.

On a hunch, Spencer placed a few popcorn kernels near the magnetron—the radar set's power tube. In minutes, the kernels popped. Intrigued, Spencer brought a tea kettle to work the next morning. He cut a hole in its side, placed a raw egg in the kettle, and aimed the opening at the magnetron. In seconds, the egg exploded, shooting bits of shell and hot yolk around the lab.

Spencer figured he was on to something. Could the magnetron—a source of short radio waves called microwaves—be capable of heating food in seconds?

Spurred on by such questions, Spencer conducted experiments with the magnetron that paved the way for a new invention. In 1953 Raytheon hit the marketplace with a magnetron-powered cooking device—the world's first microwave oven.

Qq

In 1984 zoologist Katy Payne noticed something odd while observing three Asian elephants and their calves at the Washington Park Zoo in Portland, Oregon. The air around the elephant enclosure seemed to throb, and a quiver ran through Payne's body. The strange sensation reminded her of a childhood experience when, standing close to a pipe organ at church, she had felt a similar throbbing when the lowest notes on the organ were played. *Were the elephants making sounds too low in frequency for humans to detect?* she wondered.

Curious about the phenomenon, Payne used electronic instruments to record the elephants. By analyzing the printouts, she was able to confirm her suspicions. Elephants, she learned, communicate using hundreds of different calls, many of them at frequencies well below the range of human hearing. Because the calls can reverberate over great distances, elephants can keep in contact with one another even when separated by miles.

R r

R is for Record

Standing by the elephant enclosure,
Katy Payne felt a stir.
Were the beasts sending secret messages?
Her recordings showed for sure.

S s

In 1845 explorer Sir John Franklin and his crew of 129 men sailed from England in two ships, determined to find a passageway through Canada's ice-plugged Arctic. Instead, the ships became locked in ice, and one by one the entire crew died, leaving the world a mystery to be solved. What went horribly wrong on the Franklin expedition?

In the 1980s Canadian anthropologist Owen Beattie and a team of experts scoured the Arctic, visiting the last known outposts of the Franklin expedition. On King William Island, Beattie found human bone fragments, and on the shores of Beechey Island, the frozen graves of three sailors. Tests on bone, hair, and tissue samples showed high levels of lead, likely from the solder used to seal the tins of food that the crew ate on the journey.

With Beattie's findings, part of the Franklin mystery seems solved. Lead acts like a poison, weakening the body and mind. As the men consumed the toxic food, they likely became increasingly tired, irritable, confused, and prone to diseases. Unable to think clearly and in failing health, they made terrible decisions that ultimately cost them their lives.

S is for Solve

In the windswept Arctic
three graves with hidden clues
helped solve the mystery
of Franklin's missing crew.

Monarch butterflies fascinated entomologists Fred Urquhart and his wife, Norah. From their Toronto home, they raised thousands of monarchs and studied their habits closely. Despite all their research, however, one question remained unanswered. Where did monarchs of eastern North America go each September?

In the 1940s the Urquharts began tagging monarchs, hoping to trace their migration route. With the help of volunteers, tiny pressure-sensitive adhesive labels that carried the message "Send to Zoology University Toronto Canada" were applied to the monarchs' wings before the insects were released. When tagged monarchs were discovered farther south, the Urquharts charted the information.

In 1975, after almost 40 years of research, they received an excited phone call. "We have found them—millions of monarchs!" The call came from Ken Brugger, an American engineer, who had tracked the monarchs to a mountain 240 miles (386 kilometers) from Mexico City.

The following year Fred and Norah Urquhart received the ultimate reward for their efforts when they climbed the "Mountain of Butterflies" to see firsthand the millions of butterflies who gathered there for the winter.

T is for Tag

A puzzle, those monarch butterflies.
Each winter, where did they go to stay?
Tiny tags affixed to fluttering wings
detected their secret hideaway.

In 1976, while searching for fossils near the village of Laetoli, Tanzania, paleoanthropologist Andrew Hill scooped up bits of elephant dung and playfully hurled them at another scientist. When he bent to dodge the return fire, Hill found himself face down on the ground staring at fossilized footprints in a layer of hardened volcanic mud.

Led by team leader and anthropologist Mary Leakey, the group carefully scraped away layers of encrusted soil and unearthed an astonishing find—three sets of human-like footprints 3.6 million years old. The 70 footprints ran in two parallel lines for 100 feet (30 meters) before disappearing.

The footprints seemed to tell a story: Millions of years ago a volcano erupted, spewing wet ash over the area, forcing animals to flee. Among the ancient travelers were three human-like individuals. They walked together, their feet sinking into the moist ash, leaving impressions that later hardened like cement. The discovery of the Laetoli footprints caused a stir among scientists, raising questions about evolution that beg for answers even today.

U
u

U is for Unearth

Sealed in ash, unearthed by science,
seventy footsteps in a row.
Some large, others small,
all telling about long ago.

For Friedrich Kekulé, a German chemist, the compound benzene was a problem. Other organic compounds were made of long chain of carbon atoms. In chemical reactions, whe new compounds were produced, the chains grew longer or shorter in predictable ways. No benzene. It had unique properties, behaved oddly in chemical reactions, and its molecular structure was a mystery.

One evening in 1861 Kekulé fell asleep in front of a fire and began to dream. In his dream, atoms danced like the flames in the fireplace linking first in pairs, then in longer chains. The chains twisted, turning like snakes. Suddenly one snake looped in a circle. Its head chased its own tail, grabbed it, then whirled like a spinning wheel.

Kekulé snapped awake, startled by the still-fresh vision. The snakes of his dream, he realized, provided the solution to the benzene problem. Rather than lining up in chains like other compounds, benzene's atoms had to form a circle. That was the only way to explain benzene's peculiar ways.

Kekulé's vivid dream revolutionized chemistry by giving us new understandings of chemicals and the ways that they combine.

V is for Visualize
Visions of snakes twisting,
    whirling, turning, giving chase,
inspired the circles
        that solved a troubling case.

V
V

W is for Warn

Danger! Be careful!
Rachel Carson told us all.
In graceful words, bold yet firm,
she issued a warning call.

In the 1950s Rachel Carson, an American biologist, noticed a disturbing drop in bird populations. Fewer birds were returning to nesting areas. The eggs they laid were frequently thin-shelled and fragile. The hatchlings that survived were often deformed.

Carson believed chemical pesticides were the cause. Pesticides were widely used by farmers to rid their crops of insects, but Carson was convinced that the chemicals had poisonous side effects. Birds that ate insects or drank water from pesticide-laced streams absorbed the chemicals, she argued. As toxic levels inside their bodies climbed, they died. Often, the poisons were passed on to the next generation or to other animals in the food chain.

A gifted writer, Carson put her thoughts into words and warned others of the danger. In 1962 she published *Silent Spring*, a book that described the destruction of wildlife. The book was an instant bestseller, and although the chemical industry tried to discredit Carson, the public sided with her. Eventually, laws were passed to control the use of pesticides and, inspired by Rachel Carson's words, the world entered a new age of environmental concern.

X is for eXplain

A sudden smash, a mighty blast,
a powerful cosmic show
explained the disappearance
of dinosaurs long ago.

Sixty-five million years ago dinosaurs disappeared completely. Just what killed them has been a long-standing scientific mystery.

In the 1970s Walter Alvarez, an American geologist, noticed something unusual in rock samples taken from different places. The rocks contained high concentrations of iridium, a rare metal. Just as strange was where the iridium was located. It was found in layers just above those containing dinosaur fossils.

Alvarez pointed out the unusual find to his father, Luis, a physicist. *Where had the iridium come from?* they wondered. *What, if anything, did it have to do with the extinction of the dinosaurs?*

In 1980 the Alvarez duo proposed a new theory for the extinction of the dinosaurs, one that fit the freshly uncovered facts. Sixty-five million years ago, they suggested, a massive comet or asteroid rich in iridium must have smashed into earth, spewing a cloud of iridium dust into the air. The cloud was so thick that it blocked the sun. Without sunlight, the earth turned cold. Most plants died and so, too, did many animals, the dinosaurs included.

In 1989 a giant crater almost 120 miles (193 kilometers) across was found in the Yucatan, adding support to the Alvarez explanation.

X
x

In 265 BC Archimedes, a Greek mathematician and inventor, was handed a problem. King Hieron II had ordered a new gold crown. The goldsmith swore that he had used only pure gold to make it, but Hieron was suspicious. *Had he*? Hieron asked Archimedes to find out.

For days Archimedes pondered the problem, eager to find a way of testing the crown without damaging it. Finally, he went to the public baths to relax. When he stepped into the water, the level rose, and in that instant Archimedes discovered the solution. Immersing the crown in water, he realized, and measuring how much the water rose would give him the crown's volume. Comparing the crown's weight to the weight of an equal volume of pure gold would tell him if it was made of gold. Excited, Archimedes forgot his clothes and ran down the street yelling, "Eureka!" (Greek for "I have found it!").

Distracted from his problem, Archimedes discovered not only the solution, but also a simple truth: sometimes the best ideas come when we relax, yield to the situation, and simply allow our minds to wander.

Y is for Yield

Archimedes' grand idea,
    one of his very best,
came after yielding to the moment
    and giving his poor brain a rest.

As an astronomy student at Cambridge University in England, Jocelyn Bell's job was clear: Operate a giant radio telescope; analyze the reams of data it collected; and report interesting shifts in the signal. One day in 1967 Bell detected what she later called "a bit of scruff." It was an unusually sharp burst of energy that appeared and disappeared in a steadily repeating pulse. The signal was unlike anything Bell or her adviser, Antony Hewish, had noticed before.

Puzzled, they investigated the possibilities, hoping to zero in on the source. Was there a problem with the telescope? Was it picking up interference from somewhere else? When a thorough check of the equipment showed that the signal was clearly coming from outer space, they entertained another possibility: Perhaps an intelligent life form was trying to send a message. Half joking, they named the signal "Little Green Men."

Later, three more signals were detected, each from different regions of the sky, providing Bell and Hewish with solid evidence that they had discovered not alien life, but a new type of star they called a *pulsar.*

Z is for Zero In

Could aliens be talking to us
through this pulsing energy force?
Jocelyn Bell found the answer
by zeroing in on the source.

You, the Scientist

You, the Physicist
Physics: *The study of matter and energy and the way they interact.*

In *D is for Demonstrate*, Otto von Guericke used copper spheres and horses to show air pressure's might. You can recreate his demonstration on a smaller scale using a plumber's plunger or two.

Moisten the rim of the plunger and press it against a smooth, solid surface like a tile or wood floor. Grab the handle and try pulling the plunger up and off. Not so easy, is it?

For an even greater challenge, try this with two plungers. Moisten both rims and press them together to make a tight seal. Have a partner grab one handle while you grab another. Carefully try pulling the plungers apart.

Air pressure is a powerful thing. Pressing the plunger on the floor or against another plunger squeezed out the air *inside* the plunger, creating a vacuum. The only force holding the plunger to another surface is the air pressing on its *outside*. When air seeps through the seal, the vacuum is broken, equalizing air pressure inside and out, making the plunger easy to pull apart.

You, the Environmental Scientist
Environmental science: *The study of our environment and the factors that affect it.*

In *W is for Warn*, Rachel Carson noted the effects of pesticides on our environment and alerted us to the harm caused by pollutants. Oil spills are a particularly damaging form of water pollution. Oil floats on water, kills aquatic plants and animals, leaves shorelines coated with sludge, and is difficult to clean up.

You can find out what might work in a clean-up situation with this investigation. First, create a mini oil spill by adding 5 to 10 drops of motor oil or cooking oil to an aluminum pie plate half filled with water. Now dip various products into the "oil spill" to see what mops up the mess. Try paper towel, cotton swabs, pieces of fabric, string, feathers, and other materials. How much oil is cleaned by each material? How quickly does each one work? In a large scale situation where thousands of barrels of oil are released into the ocean, how effective would these clean-up methods be?

You, the Chemist
Chemistry: *The study of substances, their properties, and the ways they interact.*

In *J is for Join*, chemist Stephanie Kwolek produced a long-chain molecule with unusual properties. Try your hand at creating a mysterious long-chain product of your own. Cover a table or other work surface with newspapers to make clean-up easier. Into a large shallow bowl, pour about ¾ cup (190 ml) of water. Stir cornstarch into the water a bit at a time until the mixture is slimy and no longer powdery. Test the mixture's thickness by tapping the surface lightly with a spoon. The mixture will be "just right" when it doesn't splatter when you hit it.

Now test the mixture's properties. Try scooping some of it up and shaping it into a ball. Let some of it drizzle through your fingers. Try slapping your hand hard and fast down on the mixture. Does this substance behave like a solid or a liquid? Or is it both?

In this gooey mixture of cornstarch and water, long chains of molecules coil together. When you squeeze the mixture, the long chains resist movement. The goop feels like a solid. When you stop squeezing, the long chains of molecules slip past each other more easily and the mixture behaves like a liquid.

Note: When you are finished with the goop, dispose of it in the trash. Don't pour it down the drain where it might clog the pipes.

You, the Microbiologist
Microbiology: *The study of microorganisms and their effects on humans.*

In *H is for Hypothesize*, Ignaz Semmelweis discovered that cleanliness helped prevent the spread of disease. You can conduct your own investigation into cleanliness with a raw potato.

With the help of an adult, cut the potato into slices and blanch them for one minute in boiling water to kill any existing microorganisms. When the slices have cooled, touch a few objects around you and rub your fingers on one of the slices to add new microorganisms to the surface. Now wash you hands with soap and water and rub your fingers on a second slice. Place each slice in separate plastic bags. Seal the bags and leave them for a few days. Which slice displays the most growth? Did soap and water make a difference?